White Sail
at Midnight

Also by Ginny Lowe Connors:

Without Goodbyes: From Puritan Deerfield to Mohawk Kahnawake

Toward the Hanging Tree: Poems of Salem Village

The Unparalleled Beauty of a Crooked Line

Under the Porch

Barbarians in the Kitchen

Anthologies Edited by Ginny Lowe Connors:

Forgotten Women: A Tribute in Poetry

Laureates of Connecticut: An Anthology of Contemporary Poetry
(with Charles Margolis)

Where Flowers Bloom: Poems of Elizabeth Park

Proposing on the Brooklyn Bridge: Poems About Marriage

To Love One Another: Poems Celebrating Marriage

Essential Love: Poems About Mothers and Fathers, Daughters and Sons

White Sail
at Midnight

⁓୭

Ginny Lowe Connors

A Publication of The Poetry Box®

Editing & Book Design by Shawn Aveningo Sanders
Cover Design by Shawn Aveningo Sanders
(cover photograph courtesy of Wyxina Tresse via UnSplash)
Author Photo by Martin Connors

ISBN: 978-1-956285-75-8
Library of Congress Control Number: 2024915527
Published in the United States of America
Wholesale Distribution by Ingram Group

Published by The Poetry Box, November 2024
Portland, Oregon, United States
ThePoetryBox.com

for my family

Contents

WHITE SAIL
AT MIDNIGHT

PENUMBRA

watching the lunar eclipse during a perigee full moon

We no longer see the shadows of bats,
their dark forms flitting bravely
against the larger night.
It seems they've all died out.

But crickets continue
to rub their little buzz saws together.
Invisibly, they're with us here tonight
        as we stand in the yard, just looking.

The moon at its perigee is round and full
as a myth. Pregnant with gold.
We watch as it tries on the cloak
of shadow cast by our planet.

Beyond us—out there, it becomes
a brilliant crescent, a folded wing
clinging to a dark and ghostly sea.
        On his last voyage

my father's eyes took on such a shine.
He'd been so large through my childhood—
until his body became a hindrance,
        began falling painfully away

and all the rages of his life followed,
quietly dissolving as if they'd never been,
though this seemed to me the time
        when anger was most called for.

[...]

Now as we watch, the moon fills out again,
turns the color of iron, color of rust.
Blood moon, its craters evident,
        wounds that will not heal.

Above it, a tiny star emits its own
sharp and focused light. Here on earth
the crickets sing. And from some other
yard, a dog lets out its long howl

so full of feeling we turn inward
for a moment, toward the primitive
in us that can't be helped.
        Then the moon emerges

from earth's penumbra.
My father, my childhood, the bats
swooping through summer evenings—
        memories projected in the dark.

Stone Harvest

1.

Fields return to forest. Years ago the farmers left,
but stone walls remember them. Miles of walls in disrepair.
What a crop of stones those farmers had! I doubt they found
beauty in them, just more hard labor. But I admire
the tumbled walls meandering in autumn's sun and shadow.
History's here among a clutter of leaves, curling vines
and fallen logs. Islands of pale lichen bloom on the stones'
rough surfaces, and soft green moss invites my touch.

2.

New England Potatoes, they called them, Satan's Seeds—
the harvest of stones heaved up by frost, by roots,
by burrowing critters each year in fields once cleared.
Another endless chore to toss them to the edges of fields.
Or pile rocks on a stone sled, let the oxen pull. Heaps of stone
turned into boundary walls, packed together
with uprooted stumps and wooden rails. Built and rebuilt
with increasing care. Men laid stones one-on-two
or two-on-one, like brickwork, capped with flat fieldstones.
Sheep high, bull strong, hog tight.

3.

The rocks are flecked with mica, mineral-streaked
with rivulets dark or light. They keep company with bindweed,
bits of wood, seeds and leaves. Rest amid ferns and pokeweed.
A few are blackened, stained perhaps by campfires centuries ago,
when bands of people roamed these woods, but had no need
for walls. Unplowed, the topsoil then was so thick with humus,
most stones stayed buried. Secrets in the soil.

[. . .]

4.

When I rest my palms against a rock, I feel the heat
it's holding. But these stones hold memory of glaciers,
huge ice sheets that scraped the earth and carved
out slabs of bedrock. The ice retreated slowly,
dropping stones along the way.

5.

Storm-tossed trees have fallen on the walls. Roots and vines
nudge them apart. Seeds fall into crevices, hidden there
by chipmunks, mice, squirrels. Young trees take root
and grow between the rocks, squeezing them apart.
The new must push against the old. Plot of every history.

6.

I touch a mossy stone tumbled near the dirt road
where I'm walking. Finger its scratches and stains.
My skin carries its own share of creases, marks and scars
after so many years of living, loving, working.
What more can I ask but that I've been of some use
before it's my turn to fall away and settle into
whatever may come next?

Driving toward the Lake

Like a long-lost friend returning
to the neighborhood, sunlight
falls into the day. Trees glow.

Pointillist paintings roll out
along the road. New leaves,
pastel yellow-greens, splotches of red buds

and a single hawk riding the thermals.

Everything's going by so quickly.
But this moment feels still. Sunlight,
the grace of trees, and looking forward.

I feel the tenderness
of new leaves while thinking
of a small lake I know, and how it waits.

The bowl of its blue, open and calm.

If ever I turn to ghost, I hope
to hold within me this single day,
Or find my way back to it.

Tangle

Early morning, the lake unruffled, not a boat in sight
        but something struggles close to shore.
Something twists in the water, thrashes—
        a snapper, large as a frying pan, but all wrong.

A dark clawed foot raises itself briefly in air.
        Could it be dying? Tangled in some rough debris?
The thing tips over; a mouth gapes upside-down.
        Setting out in the kayak, I paddle closer.

Not a single snapping turtle at all, but two
        grasping each other, wrestlers
thrashing, clasping, cleaving. I feel in my gut
        the muscular thrust of their difficult love.

Interloper, I stare, recognize the writhing,
        the absolute necessity of merging,
even as the single self struggles to keep hold.
        I too have spiraled dizzily out of myself, turned

into part of a knot that ties and unties itself until the heat
        diminishes at last. Sweat drying on our bodies,
I have shivered, pulled the blankness of a sheet over us,
        over what just happened.

Inexplicable passion, is it gone from my life,
        replaced by kind affection
cool as water? I watch the leathery necks, sharp beaks
        of two turtles turned one fantastic twisting

creature, a tangle flashing sideways in the soup
      flipping over and then—I've come too close. A splash
and they're gone, the water smoothing over,
      leaving me here, thinking, we are so alone

except for the moments we hang on,
      tangled together without reason
for a little while, a brief season, and then—
      we are not. Together we form a stubborn knot.

Near a Pond Full of Koi in November

In the language of fish, water
means world, sunlight means
gold coins falling into the purse of the world.

There are no words as pure as that light.
Look how mouths of the fish open and close,
open and close in amazement.

Leaves lift and fall: syllables
of the wind's talk. They skitter across dry grass,
veer off toward memory.

Spirals of yellow leaves, little tornadoes,
eddy in the street early one morning
as I drive to work, thinking of my father.

Mortally ill and far away, he'll never again
stroll into a sun-breezy day like this one.
You can say that moment, its gorgeous spill

of leaves, its wash of grief was years ago,
but I feel it here, right now. The yellow leaves
live beyond time's orderly fretwork.

Is there ever really a beginning and an end
or do the golden fish
simply swim round and round?

My eyes open and close, open and close,
looking inward and outward. This pond
is the color of tea, or of vanquished leaves.

But sunlight flashes, bright on fins and tails.
The golden fish keep swimming, round and round,
beyond my grasp, all dressed in graceful curves.

TREE

Coated in ice, it hums a song of remembrance—
    light breeze stroking its leaves, nest full of hatchlings.

The hatchling once dreamed of an egg,
    the perfect curving wall of it.

Egg in its nest, aroma of moss and dried mud,
    a green thread woven through twigs.

The thread from a sweater, unraveling a bit at the elbow,
    a child grown too big for it.

Sweater in cool weather, days the sun is lost
    behind a swell of silvery clouds.

Cloud billows beyond lakes and rivers, over laundry on the line,
    warm air moving slowly through sheets.

Sheet held by clothespins, by a day full of sunlight
    and shadow, the fresh smell of grass.

Clothespin in the hands of the little girl beneath the tree,
    drawing faces on the pins, dressing them with scraps of cloth.

    ir gone silver now, the girl remembers that tree, and the nest
    that fell from it one windy day, fledglings already flown.

FUGUE FOR WHAT PASSES

snowflakes	on his lashes	moments	only memory can	hold
like so many	stars	in the wilderness, our lives	flicker, flare	and spark
silent	tears	bloom briefly	like fireflies	before love disappears
flower petals	tremble and fall	fade away	in the garden	unnoticed
brief beauty	unsolvable	as dreams	I want you back	let the song continue

WHITE SAIL AT MIDNIGHT

Sometimes when I close my eyes
I see a white sail furling and unfurling,
no edges, just a tangle of light
moving beyond the known
and I believe then—maybe it's not true,
but I feel then—that you're still here—
a tremble of daring in hard rain.
The sudden flare of your spirit
comes back to me, even as the sea
scratches itself frantic, and the fog
opens up to take you in again.

My Lucky Escape from Non-Existence

If Curg had died a few months earlier,
before Hattie, my great grandmother
conceived a child

> If neighbors hadn't helped out that first winter
> when Hattie and her mother drank tea made from bark,
> and stared at the cabin's rough-hewn walls,
> considering all they'd lost

If the gun that went off had killed my grandfather
instead of his little brother

> If the man my grandfather became hadn't persisted
> after Ruby Lane said no, and no again
> until finally she agreed to step out with him
> on a blustery winter day

If the medic at Okinawa hadn't gotten to the young marine
soon enough, if the government hadn't just approved
the use of penicillin

> If my mother hadn't waited while he was overseas
> and then searched him out at the hospital
> where the girl at the front desk
> could find no record of him, no record at all

If she *had* waited
a few hours longer before getting me to the hospital
when something invisible went wrong

> If a car had barreled down the other lane
> that icy day when mine spun out of control

But I'm here.

Thirteen

Cake crumbs on the counter.
I have turned thirteen.
My skin is untouched, though zits
march across the faces of friends,
red hot, white-tipped complaints
they pinch, squeeze, dab with make-up
that conceals nothing.

In the last light of day, oak leaves
whirl down the street. Windows rattle.
Two streets over a blaring of sirens.

I have turned thirteen.
I've watched a friend walk into her new,
heavy-breasted life while boys punch
each other, leer at her, gesture.
A new bra huddles in my top drawer.
When I hold it up, my mother tells me
why bother, I've hardly the need for it.

Today the news is bigger than me, bigger
than any of us. A hurricane barrels our way.
Neighbors evacuate.

I have turned thirteen.
My friends bleed. Youngest in my class,
thin as the pause between lightning
and thunder, I am still waiting
for the changes I dread, but long for.
The lights blink off, blink on, off.

My mother sets a box of matches
on the table, three kerosene lamps,
a thermos full of coffee.

Sis chatters nervously, twisting her fingers.
Not me. I have turned thirteen.
But my innards cramp just a little
as my mother says we can't run from it,
the whirlwind hurling toward us,
trees falling in its wake.

SAYING GOODBYE TO JOHNNY MOLINA

That night he was so jazzed up—
talked faster than people could hear,
then turned to me, *Let's get out of here.*
I followed, half-running. Street lights
buzzed faintly as we passed them.
Laughter ran with us like an animal, half-wild.
The phrase *spontaneous combustion*
kept repeating itself in my head.
Oh, Johnny. Claimed a previous life
as a tightrope walker. Demonstrated,
walking heel to toe, and then with longer strides,
along the railing of a bridge.
He adored the way city lights flung themselves
over the water, rippled and gleamed.
The movement of lights on the water—
That's what a heartbeat looks like, he said.
Felt he himself was mostly made of light.
I knew he'd always be flying off into some wild space
where I could not keep up. That night
for a moment he *was* pure light
but as I looked at him, it turned red—flashing, revolving
shrieking toward us and it was I who fell
away from him toward safety
and regret.

AGGIE WAS HERE

                                    Isn't
anymore. Like any sort of weed, she
was spiky, she was trampled, nobody
claimed her. Ragwort. Thistle. She hid
behind the stadium, behind smoke, behind
purple lipstick, puffy eyes. Scratched
her name into concrete, into sand, into hours
of the night. Shouted it out but the wind
took it, the boys took it and laughed, the step-father,
the teachers with their roll books, their lists,
they never minded when she was gone.
Absent, absent, and again—absent. She
was like that cabin in the woods all covered
with vines, roof caved in, shivered windows,
room corners piled up with leaves, a few
broken dishes—you wouldn't even want
to break into it, already wrecked, already
disappearing—but there's a little china pig
on a shelf in the kitchen, and Aggie—she
wore a silver chain around her left ankle, one
small green bead on it. She was, after all,
just a girl. Choke weed, chinaberry, broken brick—
that kind of girl. Birds' nests fallen to the ground,
half-gone always. Was months ago, years, I don't know
since I last saw her, and now she's gone.
Absent again. Hardly anybody cares. But Aggie—
she was here.

Flamingoes

I slept in the next room,
waking through the night
to bring her water,

settle the white blanket
over her shoulder.
What could I do, really,

but witness her pain
or her brief escapes from it?
During my own quick

dives into darkness, dreams
came to me as flashes of light
illuminating a summer storm.

I dreamed a flock of flamingoes
the color of cherry blossoms.
A fluster of them landing

across the bay on still waters,
everything quiet but for the rustle
of wings, the opalescent air crowded

with out-flung wings, long necks
shaped like question marks.
The cloud of them settled

into pearly waters and it was dawn.
Then the dream was gone,
Hartford's dull air

blushed toward me through dusty
blinds; my gritty eyes opened and shut,
opened—I heard her stirring,

rose to go to her, and I could swear
the soft sound of wings
surrounded us.

TALISMAN FOR SPIRITUAL PROTECTION

for Derick

it wasn't the fish that mattered
catching them, I mean
it was the gentle rocking of the boat
it was the sun coming up, that slant of light
whispering across the summer morning
it was mist lifting slowly from the water
my brother carving chunks of cantaloupe
offering me bites from the tip of his knife
it was the presence of my grandfather
large and genial, someone so solid
I knew nothing could harm us
it was the low, laughing warble of loons
and the way they'd dive, disappear
surface long minutes later
in some unexpected place

there is no paradise beyond this world
even so, someone has decided
to launch more bombs
and someone else has agreed to it
suffering and grief are guaranteed
I know that now
and yet how fortunate are those, like me
who carry within them some little piece of heaven
a sweet summer morning
that returns again from the deep
a reminder, unlost
of the way the world can be

A Path through Woods

River Highlands State Park, Cromwell, CT

Let's take the day, spend it in this world of green
where human sorrows are of no account.

If trees hang their leafy headdresses over the pond,
grief has nothing to do with it. Their color

is mirrored in water. Green, green. Here water lilies
float like thin green plates. Among them a counterpoint

in pale yellow—buds just beginning to open. We turn
from the pond, follow a path through woods,

step over rocks and roots. The years
we've climbed through to get to this place.

Lush ferns crowd in from the woods, fronds
of each one articulated, tapered, delicate.

Remember the years when every weekend
was a wedding? How tender the light here,

filtered through trees. Wind whispers
through thousands of leaves and water skips

over rocks in a stream. From a hundred invisible places,
refrains of birdsong find us. Let's stay awhile.

PRESENCE

for William

Never mind that you have not yet appeared.
I know you are there, waiting.
A hummingbird hovers over the garden
and I know it's you. Yellow curtains
flutter at the window of a small room

filling with the airy scent of you.
I know you are there, waiting.
The dreams of your ancestors
are busy weaving themselves
into the whorls of your fingerprints.

A wish your mother made on a dandelion
spun off into the wind long ago.
All this time, it's been traveling toward you.
In the fine softness of your hair
the wish will take hold.

A crimson leaf lands at my feet
and I know it's you.
Somewhere a first-grade teacher
arranges the crayons, wondering which color
your eyes will be.

GIFTS

for Grayson

Your mother's heartbeat and your father's voice,
the birdsong you awaken to, the wind
at your window. And stories told, retold
shaped a little by each teller when the family gathers—
these are your inheritance.

These travel with you always
and carry you home.

All the rivers and roads, hills and trees,
the blues and greens and browns of your geographies
will flow into your signature

unique to you,
your mark on the world.

Your scrapes and bruises, the tears
your pillow gathers, and the smile
you finally see in the eyes of one who matters—
these sculpt the flesh on the bones of your face

which you turn toward others
even when you try to hide your heart.

You don't remember the stars
that watched through the night of your difficult birth,
but their light entered you.

When your breath goes slow and deep,
that long-ago light warms you

[. . .]

just as your own imperfect radiance
enters the mystery we call this world,
the one that has shaped you, and that you shape too,
every day of your ordinary, quite extraordinary life.

Special Delivery

In 1913 parcel post service was introduced and for a while children could be mailed to relatives, with stamps attached to their clothing. Soon afterward, a new regulation forbidding this practice was passed.

The letter carrier leans just a little,
slightly to the right. He leans
balancing the weight of the mailbag,
its strap over his left shoulder.

A toddler stares from the canvas pouch,
moonfaced, his cheeks little apples.
He stares, wondering mutely, *Is this how it is to be?*
Handed over from one giant to another to another?

The cap on his head is already too small
but the world is big, full of big people
who place a cap on your head, and hand you over.
Over to the next person, the next thing.

Even today it's easy to feel that way.
Life has a way of packing you up, handing you over,
the cap on your head a little too small.
Nothing to be done about it.

GAS, 1940

after Edward Hopper

Instead of a flag
      on the tall pole, a white sign
            swings back and forth, Mobil gas

and Pegasus poised
      to leap past this bright emptiness,
            fly beyond this road edged with sand

back to the realm of his birth,
      that place wondrous strange.
            Anything can happen there.

In an instant a woman turns
      into a tree, a gargoyle, a fly.
            A young man buckles his sandals,

stuffs a blade in his satchel
      and follows the hero road
            to death or immortality.

Pegasus could fly off
      past that huddle of trees
            into a story. His wings are spread—

but something stops him.
      Every time.
            It's the man, his loneliness,

the mortality of his bald head,
     the way he leans into
          the bubble-headed gas pumps

as if they could save him.
     Across the narrow road the trees
          are dark and thick—they crowd

in close. The man retreats
     to a small white hut, straightens
          the candy, freshens the coffee,

waits for the next stranger
     to arrive. He glances up,
          watches the road darken.

Rebecca's Alphabet

is stitched on a scrap of linen
a bit larger than my hand. Homely little piece
passed down through the years.
Holding it, I hear the echo
of a small girl's voice. Listen.
She hums, complains, shakes her head, starts over.
She hopes for her mother's approval.
Two centuries ago, Rebecca embroidered this sampler,
a practice piece, its small letters rendered
in four neat rows. Each stitch a tiny raised nugget
of careful intent. The thread might once have been gold.
She tried hard, but a yellow bird flew past the window,
and the cat's tail twitched. She dropped her cloth
and started again. And then there were two letter **O**'s.
L – M – N – O – O –P…
Like two wide open eyes. Two mouths exclaiming.
I notice the **B** and the **C** are slightly stained.
K stretches out like a person walking
and **X** resembles a butterfly.
The letters of her name are even smaller than the rest,
but the **R** the **A** and another **A** are gracefully looped.
Rebecca Ann Applewhite.
My great-great-great grandmother.
A is for ancestor   or Ann   or Applewhite.
R is for remnant   or remembrance   or Rebecca.
With this alphabet, her story begins.

For My Daughter After Her Last Appointment with the Orthodontist

The caterpillar, yellow and black, nudges along,
its beauty seldom recognized. It accepts
the generosity of the milkweed, chewing
and chewing, until it becomes impossible
to ignore the strange compulsion
to zip itself into a sleeping bag,
pale shell that hangs, precarious, from a twig.
It doesn't consider the danger, just falls
into a sort of dream as the sun sets and rises,
as rain falls, as breezes sweep over it.
It hangs, wobbling a little, until a crack
forms in its protective shell. A new body
begins its slow unfurling. The thin cocoon,
faithful shelter, breaks open.
Air whispers to wings. Wings!
They vibrate softly with strange urgency.
Maybe it's instinct. Possibly hope
that grants this one the courage
to shed its old life, leap into flight.

Pack Horse Librarian

The Pack Horse Library Project was a WPA program that employed women to travel on horseback or mule to deliver library books to people in remote areas of the Appalachian Mountains.

They call her The Book Woman. A hundred miles or so each week, she and her horse, Bonny Bee, climb hills, splash through creeks, travel with their load of books over rocky paths. The roadcut rises high, the steep bank eroded by runoff. Eastern Kentucky. Pay is 28 dollars a month. Teacher pauses class when the children begin to shout, *The Book Woman is here! The Book Woman!* Fourteen books handed out, twelve collected back. On horseback, The Book Woman fords Cut Shin Creek, her feet raised high—the water's bone-chilling. Brings the recipe scrapbook to Katie Block, sixteen years old and newly married. Burboo with Mashed Potatoes. Green Bean Casserole. Stack Cake. Supposing the girl can get the food, she'll try these out. Visits Hal Barton, laid up with a gunshot wound. Reads to him, leaves him a magazine: *True Detective*. She's got a copy of *Huckleberry Finn* for Jon McAllister. He's read two other Twain books—wants more. Book Woman crosses a deer track winding up from the creek bed. Hears the soft whistle of a meadowlark, spies one perched on a twig, feathers ruffled by breeze. Visits Granny Smithers, gives her another reading lesson. Continues on. Pauses to watch a swirl of golden leaves fling themselves to the muddy earth. She stops by Margaret Alred's cabin, reads Bible passages to her. The old woman is half-blind and her cabin's cold. She's grateful for company. Book Woman rekindles the stove, shares a bite of cornbread, a sip of huckleberry tea. Must start back.

Wind's up. Clouds rolling in.
The horse shakes its head, shivers.
Eight miles to go.

A Girl of Maiduguri

In Maiduguri, Nigeria, a place at war with Boko Haram, people are afraid of girls and young women.

The girl walks in silence. She doesn't want to kill anyone.
Walks toward the crowded market, but doesn't want to kill anyone.

She resisted the fighter who tried to marry her. Rape her. No!
You'll be sorry, he spat. No! She doesn't want to kill anyone.

Everything so heavy. Her memories. The heat. Explosives
wrapped around her. She doesn't want to kill anyone.

People fear young women now, especially those
who walk alone. They wonder, will she kill anyone?

Childhood games not long ago. Tinko Tinko, clap clap.
Fire on the Mountain, the circles move. No need to kill anyone.

She was a daughter, a sister. Who is she now? Captive? Cipher?
Almost-flame? Almost-ghost? Girl who doesn't want to kill anyone.

In the market, laughter. White teeth flashing. Baskets piled high
with yams, plantains, tomatoes. She doesn't want to kill anyone.

Her name began with G, but it's falling away. She's just a body
wired with a bomb. Who will help her? She doesn't want to kill anyone.

They Follow Me

Even here, even now, a Sunday morning at the lake—
in the thousand points of fiery light

jumping up and down on the unstill water, uncatchable,
mesmerizing, various, all the small elf lights making one

field of scintillating light—my students suddenly appear:
restless, chattery, overflowing with bluster

or timidly emitting that inner glow so mysterious,
untouchable and luminous that it keeps me returning

again and again to their exhausting world—
near-adolescents packed like a drawerful of mismatched socks

into a single classroom. I run away. Close my eyes,
open them in a new place—discover I've been followed.

Sun's got the whole lake dancing with light
but only part of me can attend. The classroom

won't let go. Even kids who will be plain one day
are beautiful now as they change daily, becoming

themselves as they try on new ways of being.
Every day they look toward me, expecting something.

I pour myself into the classroom and then—retreat.
Weekends I think water, I think trees, escape.

The young are on their way to somewhere else.
I want simply to wave them on their way

but they say no, they drive right through me,
mark me with tire tracks, leave me panting,

breathing in their exuberant exhaust.

Rodrigo Fails to Meet
the Learning Objective

Numbers wheel across the whiteboard,
swerve of swallows arcing suddenly over the bridge

into the evening sky. He remembers that sky
from last night, settling over the city
in its startling hues of indigo and gold.

Without even trying, he memorized the birds,
their geometry of appear and disappear,
feathered unison in the fading light.

But right now Rodrigo doesn't have the answer—
the integer, the positive number, the solution,
the refrain. All he has is the feeling

that chairs have nothing to do with living (yet here he sits),
that figures are meant to be moving
and that dance, although it's not for boys,

not for boys like him, would be a better way to answer.
He knows this in all the muscles of his body,
in all the colors of his mind … but how to say it?

Rodrigo squirms in his seat, concentrates
on a wasp knocking itself against the window.
The light's become a slippery plane, hard, indecipherable

but still the wasp keeps climbing and buzzing, feeling
its way along, looking for a way out.

She Talked to Me Once

but now she won't open the door.
Speaks only to the dead, who sit on her bed in their blue capes,
  their starry crowns, speaking their language of chant,
sigh and creak. When lights flicker, when the chair tips over,
  it's the dead dropping by again, looking for a beaded purse,
a fan made entirely of feathers. I wonder, is she lonely?
  For years she was lost among the living. Talked to me once,
but worries now I'll interfere. Sprinkles salt on the window sill
  to keep me and the crows away. Prefers the solace
of her slippers. Wooly pets, they follow her around, soft and forgiving.
  Sometimes a raft of bills rattles through her mail slot.
Glossy little windows on the envelopes. Hieroglyphics inside. She watches
  the stove lick their wrappers, turn them all to ash. Company?
A few cinders wander the room, looking for someplace to land. And bits
  of the ceiling rain down—this happens often. She talked to me
once of a sky of confetti, how the bright bits landed on her hair,
  her shoulders, and on all the drunken, smiling figures in the street.
When was that? I don't know. Her hair was thick then, orange and frizzy.
  She had a navy pin dot dress. But her outside self never matched
her inside self. So she let it go. Took to staring at that painting,
  the one with the two women, her great Aunt Zenobia
and Marybelle, the sister. It's them all right, she insists, them thinking
  that flimsy whatayacallit—parasol—will save them.
She told me this once. When she speaks now, it's only to the dead.

THE MURDERER'S MOTHER WONDERS

No one else seemed to notice
the density of him.
Even when he was a baby

portable as a football, he was a bag of cement.
I dragged myself through the hours
weighted down by him.

It was my secret,
the way I took the gift of him
as a burden. In the baby's crying jags

I heard my grandfather's unending sorrow
calling out to me
as the air turned purple and sharp.

Dishes teetered in the cupboard.
His limbs flung out in sudden startles,
as if to ward off disaster

and I was always unprepared.
That his fingers were tiny spatulas
made his father proud. They were the digits

of tool and dye makers, and before that
the tanners who gave my husband
his family name. He was ours, all right,

so why was he such a little stranger,
turning from me after he fed to puke a little
and then to belch, purr, fall into a twitchy slumber?

I should have loved him more.
He was always ravenous.
Just before he'd latch onto the breast

a little growl
would come from him, low in the throat.
He could have been a wolf cub.
Or I might have been something cornered
in a cave, an alley, in a darkness
that had no words.

Something basic I was lacking

I tried to pin on him; that's the truth,
now isn't it?

Give him to me my husband's dark-lipped aunt
demanded one day when I was peckish,
exhausted, sore at heart.

Unreasonable me, I never liked that woman
so I held my lumpkin closer,
but still she took him—

sent him into some kind of miraculous sleep
that lasted ten hours.
When I woke at last from my own

surrender, head thick as a melon,
eyes aching and hot
I rushed in to check on the little man

and there he was, fine as he'd ever be,
smiling up at me with a small, secret smile
that made me fall into the rocker and cry.

THE OLD HALFBACK

after Donald Hall's "Olives"

What can the old obese halfback do
but wheeze upstairs to sleep
beside his cheerleader, who turns away

with a murmur? The hip replacement
she'll be in for soon—just the idea of it
makes her restless and fussy.

Clutching his pillow instead of a ball,
instead of her fallen breast, he submits
to a thunder of dreams. Herd of bulls

pounding the earth, breath steaming,
a roar like trains or waterfalls rushing
from mountains that close in, and then

the cliff—every time a fresh surprise
and the falling, the falling, with never
any landing but the shock of waking up

in this undreamt-of life, the job
any sleepwalker could do, the daughter
with her problems. Humility the toughest

uniform to wear; just lately he's begun
to try it on. A series of stupidities interrupted
by small pools of light—this is his life.

Still, he reaches for the old fortitude,
the decency to stick with a pretty good woman
though her pompom days are over.

He's not the type to sit crying into a beer.
Gravity's claimed him and if *gravitas*
isn't quite within his reach

at least he lumbers through the fallen world
with a tenacity even his hard-assed old coach
might've cheered.

Landscape with Thorns and Caterpillars

give me rain on the campfire   give me
those uncertain sparks   off-and-on lights at twilight
my doubts   thicken into thorn bushes   complaints
become a shower of stones   this fickle landscape
cracked earth, rock, weeds   it suits me
I do what must be done   but the trail of my laziness
is silver slime   the snail in its thin shell
retains an innocence   but I   let's remember
it's human to err   the syrup of gossip is sweet
trees infested with caterpillars   don't look
too deeply into the glass   that glare
good fortune of others   something to celebrate   I never
meant jealousy   field of poison ivy, glossy and mean
how it spreads   one needs to be polite   one needs
to drop the black anchor   don't talk to me
of constancy   when did you ever   if I close my eyes
the badger caught in a snare   its face with three white markings
curled lip   leave it, leave it   how useless
my anger is   circling the earth   comet, tail on fire

THE WOODS IN NOVEMBER
OF A DIFFICULT YEAR

We walk through an hour of late autumn light
on a wooded path, my grown daughter and I,
through leaf mold and shadow.

Heavy twists of vine, thick as ropes
wrap trees to the point of strangulation.
Tumbled boulders edge the trail.

It's a bleak season: illness sweeps
through the world, cutting down millions
and there's family we haven't seen in months.

We wonder at a gnarl of barbed wire
embedded in the remnants of an old stump,
piercing the heart of splintered wood.

November's song is the dry rasp of leaves,
kinder than the voices we leave behind
that shout grievous lies from high offices.

My daughter's voice is subdued.
I used to believe in something we called America,
she says, plucking a thorn from her sleeve.

Our talk, then, shifts closer to home
and we reflect on betrayals
that have split our own family.

We're not immune from the falling away.
A woodpecker keeps knocking

[. . .]

but we fail to see a single bird, just trees,

many of them fallen, others
barely upright, rough bark loosening,
insect holes cratering trunks.

The land is November-sere,
everything waiting, it seems
for some final catastrophe or revelation.

Tangles of bittersweet clutter the woods
and November smells like loneliness
but we have this quiet hour together.

We celebrate a tiny tree, thin blessing
sprouting from a rotting stump.

HER EYES

ICU nurse during the pandemic

Above the mask, behind the face shield,
her eyes are huge; they're falling out of her head.
They're red-rimmed, gritty, glassy.

She yearns to close them. Open or closed,
there is so much she can't unsee.
It's required of her—to witness

this human devastation. And will anything she does
make a difference? She tightens the mask.
If she could walk near the river, gaze quietly at trees,

at sky. But the clouds she looks at, day after day,
float to the surface of films held up to a lightboard.
Lungs filled with confetti. Ground glass.

Fourteen hours at the hospital
and tomorrow promises more of the same.
So many people offer their desperation.

She sees the loneliness of their terror
and what is she to do with it?
They won't see hers.

When one young man looked toward her
he wheezed out, *Please!*
I don't want an astronaut. I want my mother.

[. . .]

Finally home, she glances in the mirror.
Her eyes are rags, barely fastened to her face.
They look like wounds, bandages unraveling.

She stands in her shower's cascade,
unable to wash away scenes she's witnessed,
fears she's felt, all the things she cannot fix.

Two Years In

February, 2022

Ice clogs the gutters and coats the driveway.
That slick shine. Just another false promise.
10,000 lives lost to the virus in our own small state,
but everyone's tired of hearing about it. Last week
we had a day so full of sun, we remembered
the idea of spring. A pair of robins appeared
like valentines sent to the wrong address.
A thousand miles away, my son survived a crash.
Six-car pile-up. Mangled metal strewn across the highway.
The hard shell of his car cracked open. But not his skull.
Not his skull. He walked away, just a little bruised.
It wasn't till later he started to shake. That night,
he dreamed of flying. Arms spread wide. I wonder
how close to earth he flew. If he could see lakes and rivers,
or up north, snow melting and re-freezing into hard,
crystalized ridges and hummocks. Did he see the widow
walking her little dog, the school crossing guard in her mask,
holding up the sign that says STOP? I wasn't there; couldn't
warn him not to fly too far. I live my life grateful and terrified.
Sometimes the best I can do is to wrap my hands
around a cup of coffee on a cold, clear morning.
Right now, my daughter's son stretches out on the carpet
using blocks to build a race track with jumps, bridges, false turns.
It's like a maze, he says, you have to figure out
which way to go, and sometimes you guess wrong.

Remembering Anastasia

Anastasia Yalanskaya, Ukraine, March 2022

When the sky refused to stay whole,
when it burst into flames,
a migraine of bombs and missiles
three days in a row, they urged her
to evacuate. She ran
her fingers through thick brown hair.
Insisted, *I want to help.*

You, though, you feel helpless
and distant. And there's dinner to make.

She said, *We are not afraid*
as black boots commanded the streets,
ordinary streets, neighborhood streets,
where a cat sat in the window of a brick home,
half the roof blown away.

It's past time to get out, she was told.
But the children, she said.
40 children left without food
at the daycare center. They clapped
when she arrived with bread and cucumbers,
pirozhki, diapers, blankets, even
a cannister of milk, a carton of cookies.

If you have children, aren't they well-fed?
Maybe they're grown.
Perhaps you have a daughter,
20 years old, 25, blooming with health
and confidence. Like Anastasia.

Now it's really time to go,
they told her, and she admitted
she was tired. *They blew up the bridge,*
the one I walked on yesterday. We'll have to
find another way. What's to be done
with one so stubborn?

Maybe you've said that about your own child,
when she was three and refused
to wear anything but her rubber boots and tattered tutu
day after day.

Anastasia's clothes were dusty,
but her smile was hard to resist.
We've run out of food for dogs at the shelter,
someone told her. Three days they've gone without.
For years a feisty little dog,
one ear up, the other undecided,
trotted at her heels. Curled up near her
at night. So she scoured the city, found a way
to get boxes of kibble to the shelter.
The dogs were fed.
And then ...

Well, you know the rest.
This is a war poem.

WHEN OMENS FOUND US

after Adolph Gottlieb's Omen for a Hunter

even after five nights of moonlight silvering the pond	we weren't prepared for the earthquakes, the flooding	when finally we looked at ourselves	a small beam of light pierced the darkness
our hearts went unrepaired— arrows we'd fired years ago returned to wound us	in fabulous masks, we tried to chase away our terrors	we were haunted by dreams of feathers falling	we faced the hardest questions, felt their sting
rivers ran ocher with the poisons we'd made	we retreated, we retreated	from a bird called Desolation	while our spears remembered their life as trees

Earth Pot with Tokens

after the painting by Virginia Dehn

She spent a life
translating inner landscapes
into the language of paint, fabric, and clay.

In this painting of an earthen pot,
every color shimmers with other colors,
like the complications of thought.

Layers of texture
suggest hands. Touch.
Fingertips learning the world.

Hands of a potter from centuries past.
And her own careful hands, coaxing a vision
into something that might stay.

Though she herself
would refuse to stay much longer.

I look to her paintings for clues.
Find colors I cannot name.
Find scraps of linen, grains of sand,
tiny clay figures.

In this painting, fragments
scored with cuneiform
flake away from the vessel.

[. . .]

Cryptic messages.
Unreadable, unstable.
Urgent.

And in the ground
above which the pot seems to float,
tiny buried objects, little bones,
beads or amulets,

or the scrim of stars
fallen from a great distance.

History of Our Travels

Once we lived among animals.
We *were* animals.

Our thin fur, our wariness. Appetites.
Our whistles, groans and growls.

Once we sheltered among trees.
We could hear the wind

before it arrived. We bent down
and listened as seeds cracked open,

as tiny leaves unfurled. We gathered
plants. Prayed to them and for them.

Then we yanked ourselves away,
hardly noticed colors of the sky

its soft blue tenderness, its sorrow.
Now we go and go and go, never

looking where, never touching dirt.
We believe in our own dominion

We keep going, keep going
toward some place we cannot see.

Winter, Almost

The surface freezes
           and unfreezes.
This is what doubt looks like.

The lake is black and silver, shields of ice
arranged in rounded archipelagoes,
       darkness between them,

sheen of moisture riding them.
On the ragged shore of doubt,
       pale shafts of sunlight

creak through shadows, form a restless beauty
       like the swirls of ice out there,
cracked and burnished, trying to take hold.

Season of Ghost Apples

The gustnado was a surprise, coming as it did after a few fine days of Indian Summer. Spinning and spinning, leaves, twigs, and dirt into a spiral that stretched up and spread out in a thick, harsh swirl, it called the darkening sky down. Huge clouds. Hard, cold rain. Not a month later the ground seemed to explode, booming and banging—it was frost quakes. Icy groundwater freezing, expanding, pressing at rocks below. The ground popped like gunfire, and the sound boomeranged. Then, after days of gray weather: thunder sleet. Rain turned to bullets of ice that pinged hard on the windows and clattered on the ground. The sky let loose with thunder and lightning that had no business arriving uninvited and unannounced—summer was long over. It was loud, crazy-loud. Tree branches and sidewalk iced up. A strange landscape. Later, of course, came bombogenesis, a blizzard that buried the state and kept on going. Trees down, power out, snow so high even the plows couldn't get through. Second night, the wind died down, though it kept on snowing. The world suddenly went quiet. What country was this? What century? And how would it all be remembered? A painting, an opera, an ornament?

icy spheres left behind
frozen apples turn to mush
slip through the crystalline globes—
ghost apples in the orchard

TREES OF FARMINGTON AVENUE

have the knack for patience.
This early in March, their branches are leafless.
But it's now we can see the nests they hold,

big leafy ones for squirrels, smaller woven ones
for songbirds. We long to hear that music again.
Instead, there's the rumble and sigh

of cars and busses—braking, continuing on.
A road crew's lopped branches from a red oak.
Its roots quietly persist in heaving the sidewalk up.

A grayish, papery sphere, slightly tattered,
sways from a tree on the corner.
Hornets' nest. Abandoned, but abiding.

An ambulance wails down the avenue
and I wonder briefly if it's someone I know.
This tree I'm approaching has no nests,

no leaves, no slowly unraveling paper dome.
Instead it blooms with three plastic bags
caught up in its knobby limbs. They billow and flap

with a strange energy. Suffer the wind.
Across the street, near no tree at all
is a shuttered building, shred of news

blown against the iron fence, and a man
holding a sign, holding out a hand, holding on.
He's been there a long time

like the winter we gave no thought to last spring.

BELIEF

Birds make you as happy as money, researchers report.
Especially their sounds. I believe it. I can't believe
in heaven, but if there *were* a heaven, it would include
birdsong. The finch's whistles, the titmouse's whee-oo,
whee-oo, the woodpecker's warble and tock tock tock.

The rain has stopped. Stars appear. A luna moth
has fastened itself to the screen door, night messenger
the color of leaves. Its wings are delicate fans.
I wonder if it remembers its past life in a blanket of silk.
Its eye spots stare blindly. *Thank you for coming,* I say.

There's nothing quite like the spill of moonlight
across the dark waters of a lake. Astronauts say the moon
is a dusty stone. My grandma says it swells a woman's
pregnant belly. Tonight I believe the moon
is a pomegranate, and stars are a scattering of its seeds.

Hosanna

I wonder if the children in the rowboat
will remember this particular morning,
the lake restlessly turning over
a thousand scintillating points of light
except for one calm, mirror-like swathe
through which the man rows calmly,
his boy and girl looking out
from the prow of the wooden boat,
while all around them little flames
move across the lake, never arriving
anywhere except into this moment
which seems to me closer to heaven
than any other thing that man or God
might possibly contrive.

I Present This Summer's Spiderweb Award to the Orb Spider on Our Deck

Never mind that your web is slightly tattered.
      It's survived a long scorching summer.
           Over a foot in diameter, it stretches
      from railing to railing. This morning's brief rain
has left it beaded with tiny prisms. It takes
      the prize, this jeweled mosaic, shivering slightly
           in a breeze that wafts up from the lake.
      The silken lines hold. Each one from your own
           compact body. How did you learn
this intricate geometry? When you hatched
      in springtime, your mother was gone.
           You're hiding now, but come evening,
you'll be climbing all over the web, making repairs,
      wrapping up insects that stumble in.
           I've watched you do it. Watched you
      coordinate your eight legs and eight eyes
with ease as you elevator up and down
      the gossamer strands. Once again tonight,
           you'll dangle, swing, and clutch.
When an owl calls out from the old pine, you'll crouch
      on the web, feeling those deep vibrations
           as they tremble through each silken thread.

SNAG

snag: a standing tree that is dead or decomposing

You endure the thick vines snarling
your trunk and dangling like drunken snakes.
And the wind, you endure that too,
and the jagged breakage
where your largest branch snapped off.
The rough armor of your bark is mottled,
grooved, burled. You stand firm
but are softening within—from a hollow
at your base a litter of wood dust spills.
The moon has rested in your branches.
You are familiar with the thin light of stars,
the soft whuff of an owl's wings.
Now beetles and ants inhabit you.
Woodpeckers arrive to feast on them
and you allow it. In a cavity ten feet up,
you shelter a nest. Within the earth,
your roots reach out toward others.
Everything, everyone is connected.
It appears you're slowly unmaking yourself,
but that's not right, really. You're finding
yourself in others. As one must do.

LIKE SMOKE

A large fish jumps, transcending, momentarily
its boundary of water. Across the inlet
something crackles, licking at twilight—
bonfire on the shore. The dance of its orange
flames in black water a flare of surprise,
bright reflection on a dark canvas.

Fire on water, simple fact, brilliant dream.
A plume of smoke billows up behind the trees,
loses itself in the breath of an autumn night.
Half clouded over, the moon is rising too, not quite full.
Every existence a process of becoming.

It's when I let go of myself, dissolve
into the fabric, that I become most myself,
become night air pressing at window glass, become
the moth with its dusty wings.
Flame leaping across water, moon
with its cloak of cloud, those are what I am,
and I am the fish, too, briefly flying.

BEYOND

Once we accept our limits, we go beyond them.
—Albert Einstein

We are mere matter.
Every second of our lives,
parts of us transform—
our atoms, our memories.
Day to day, year to year
fragments of us disappear,
while the relentless rush
of energy that is our universe
pushes out and away,
trying to find its limits.

We are mere matter,
but wonder keeps escaping
the brittleness of bones.
Muscular and tender,
it hurls itself
into the night sky,
the great dark,
where comets wheel by
and pinpoints of light
travel eons to find us.

Nights the Moon Can't Be Found

You are not so alone as you imagine.
Who has never been lost?
The thing to do is keep going,
even in the darkness, even in the rain.
Summer mornings will arrive on schedule,
the trees filled with light, inhabited
by birds. Their sweet, jazzy trills of song.
You say they know nothing of grief.
Isn't that why we need them? To remind us
of what comes before, what comes after
nights the moon can't be found.
Not far into the woods, a fawn
rests in a circle of ferns. You saw one once,
remember? — before it had learned fear.
Sunlight filtered through the canopy of trees
as the fawn took a step toward you.
And your breathing became the breath of trees.

GREEN SEA

after Milton Avery

A dark lunge of green folds over a softer green,
which flows into a green so pale, so calm
it's nearly translucent, the petals of a rose
some might call white. Each spread interrupted

by long curls of restless turquoise.
I just want to keep looking
as the colors move forward and back.
It's the sea rolling toward shore

or a deep grief that swells and fades but won't fall away
or a dream that washes over me and stays and stays
through one long day and into the next.
It's a green glass bottle my grandmother filled
with tiny paper scrolls: a wish,
a complaint, sorrow, secret.

Within each of us, another sea,
audible in the sounds of a newborn's heart:
whoosh, whoosh, whoosh.
All of us holding our own seas.
Mortality calling out to the eternal.

I put my grandmother's secrets,
and the dream that follows me for days,
and the grief of my ancestors,
the grief of my descendants—

all these things I bundle into a ship
made of tigerwood and moonstone.
Push it out into the deep green sea.
I watch it as it goes, thinking how we—
all of us—must disappear. But how green
the sea that carries us.

ON THE INFINITUDE OF THE UNIVERSE

after Jackson Pollock's Convergence

millions of suns, their flares, storms, gases streaming out
orbits and swerves, explosions, streaks
of comets, their long tails of dust
and then the pull of black holes
more terrifying than any addiction
I'm a micro-speck in this combustible
ever-expanding wowness

and the music of the galaxies—
I swear I heard it one night
after fireflies extinguished their lights
o, it rocks me, all of it

colors hurtling within and beyond
the way they spark, flash, and disappear
in some small way I'm part of it
this unfathomable wildness

I want to reach out, take in the dark matter
and the light traveling through, beyond
my perception, but when I try to grasp
the infinitude of the universe
it's chaos
until I go deep, deep, deeper
into the great silence

ACKNOWLEDGMENTS & GRATITUDE

Grateful acknowledgment is made to the editors of the following publications where these poems first appeared:

21ˢᵗ Century Plague: Poetry from a Pandemic (University Professor Press): "Her Eyes"

Buddhist Poetry Review: "Driving Toward the Lake"

Cardinal House Poetry (Flying Horse Press): "Penumbra"

Connecticut Literary Anthology (Elephant Rock Productions): "Like Smoke" and "Season of Ghost Apples"

Connecticut Poets Respond (video): "History of Our Travels"

Crosswinds Poetry Journal: "Belief," "The Old Halfback," "She Talked to Me Once," "Rodrigo Fails to Meet the Learning Objective," and "Landscape with Thorns and Caterpillars"

Entropy: "Flamingoes"

Fish Anthology 2013 (Fish Publishing): "Tangle"

Innisfree Poetry Journal: "on the infinitude of the universe" and "Talisman for Spiritual Protection

inScribe: "Gifts"

Light: A Journal of Photography & Poetry: "Presence"

The Main Street Rag: "Snag"

NFSPS Founder's Award, first prize: "The Murderer's Mother Wonders"

NFSPS Poetry Society of Texas Award, first prize: "Gas,1940"

North American Review: "White Sail at Midnight"

Nostalgia Press, Heart Poetry Award, first prize: "The Woods in November of a Difficult Year"

Passager, Passager Poetry Contest First Prize for a group of poems: "Aggie Was Here," "A Girl of Maiduguri," and "Near a Pond Full of Koi in November"

Poems Illuminating Art (video): "When Omens Found Us"

Poem Central: Word Journeys with Readers and Writers (Stenhouse Publications): "They Follow Me"

Rappahannock Review: "Packhorse Librarian"

Stained: An Anthology of Writing About Menstruation (Abe Books): "Thirteen"

Tabi Po Poetry Literary Magazine: "Trees of Farmington Avenue"

Verse Virtual: "Nights the Moon Can't Be Found" and "Saying Goodbye to Johnny Molina"

Waking Up to the Earth: Connecticut Poets in a Time of Global Climate Crisis (Grayson Books): "Stone Harvest"

Wordpeace: "Remembering Anastasia"

Your Daily Poem: "Hosanna" and "Special Delivery"

The title poem, "White Sail at Midnight" has been set to music as a mezzo-soprano/piano aria, composed by Sarah Marze, and is forthcoming from North Star Music.

My deepest thanks go to early readers of some of these poems, for their feedback and their friendship. particularly the Pips: Christine Beck,

Sherri Bedingfield, Debbie Gilbert, Pat Hale, Joan Hoffman, Nancy J. Kerrigan, Julia Paul, and Elaine Zimmerman, as well as members of the Farmington Valley Chapter of CPS.

Further appreciation goes to Wyn Cooper, for his astute comments on the manuscript.

I offer grateful acknowledgment to the Connecticut Audubon Society and its Trail Wood residency program, which allowed me to stay in the former home of naturalist/writer Edwin Way Teale, to walk the trails there, and to have uncluttered time to work on this collection.

EARLY PRAISE

White Sail at Midnight is a quietly comprehensive book of poems. Connors' adept use of language and syntax shifts natural paradigms and teases out the extraordinary in the everyday: the sky becomes a "bowl of blue," and "bittersweet" becomes a double entendre of nightshade and sorrow. Whether rendering meditation on the poignantly perplexing beauty of impermanence, measuring time and passage in pastoral images, or considering her worldview through the lens of the Connecticut landscape, each poem is startling and fresh in its method and presentation.

—Antoinette Brim-Bell, Connecticut State Poet Laureate

A quality of attentive wonder charges and characterizes the beautifully crafted, thought-provoking poems in Ginny Connors's *White Sail at Midnight*. Through these meditations about personal experiences, relationships, and the lives of others, Connors explores the reality and mystery of existing in this world and universe. Acknowledging that "we are so alone" and that "suffering and grief are guaranteed," the poet shows a life lived "grateful and terrified"—one that soberly faces "you have to figure out/ which way to go, and sometimes you guess wrong," and at the same time, one that is awed by the world's "restless beauty...trying to take hold," and "mortality calling out to the eternal." Here is the earnest and candid work of a seasoned poet.

—Aaron Caycedo-Kimura, author of *Common Grace*

". . . this jeweled mosaic, shivering slightly/ in the breeze that wafts up from the lake. . ."

Connors is describing an orb spider's web, the beads of rain on it shimmering in windblown sunlight, but the image serves as an apt emblem for this collection of poems about being mortal in a mortal world.

Finely woven, out in the open, Ginny Lowe Connors' poems catch the momentary light and shadow of transformations and survivals, sorrows and healings. Connors meets the world, "this unfathomable wildness," with gratitude, terror, and wonder. Her poems are finely observed, deeply felt, offered to us with a quiet generosity. What can we do but meet them with a deep bow?

—Margaret Gibson, Connecticut Poet Laureate Emerita,
author of *The Glass Globe*

ABOUT THE AUTHOR

Ginny Lowe Connors is the author of five previous poetry collections, the most recent of which is *Without Goodbyes: From Puritan Deerfield to Mohawk Kahnawake* (Turning Point, 2021). Among her awards are the Sunken Garden Poetry Prize, Atlanta Review's Grand Prize, and the Founders Award, sponsored by the National Federation of State Poetry Societies. She was named "Poet of the Year" by NEATE (New England Association of Teachers of English). In 2018 she was named the winner of *Passager's* annual Poetry Contest. Essays and book reviews she's written have appeared in such publications as the *Hartford Courant, Baltimore Review, New York Journal of Books, Switchback*, and *North American Review*. In 2023 Connors was Writer in Residence at Trail Wood, former home of naturalist Edwin Way Teale. She holds an MFA in poetry from Vermont College of Fine Arts. As publisher of her own press, Grayson Books, Connors has edited a number of poetry anthologies, including *Forgotten Women: A Tribute in Poetry*. A Board Member of the Connecticut Poetry Society, she is co-editor of *Connecticut River Review*.

About The Poetry Box®

The Poetry Box, a boutique publishing company in Portland, Oregon, provides a platform for both established and emerging poets to share their words with the world through beautiful printed books and chapbooks.

Feel free to visit the online bookstore (thePoetryBox.com), where you'll find more titles including:

Inside, Outside by Kirsten Morgan

The Squannacook at Dawn by Richard Jordan

Reading Wind by Carol Barrett

Journey of Trees by Susan Landgraf

Vitals & Other Signs of Life by David A. Goodrum

Lamplight by Cathy Cain

Acceleration Due to Gravity by Heikki Huotari

Life in No Ordinary Time by Laurel Feigenbaum

Field Notes from an Illusion by Lois Levinson

What She Was Wearing by Shawn Aveningo Sanders

When All Else Fails by Lana Hechtman Ayers

This Is the Lightness by Rachel Barton

Self Dissection by Amelia Diaz Ettinger

The Beautiful One's Ark by Sher A. Schwartz

A Bit Left of Straight Ahead by Kim Peter Kovac

Rescue Dogs by Fred Zirm

and more . . .

Milton Keynes UK
Ingram Content Group UK Ltd.
UKHW050645261124
451531UK00026B/231

9 781956 285758